ELECTRICITY

Is Everywhere

by Nadia Higgins

illustrations by Andrés Martínez Ricci

Content Consultant:

Paul Ohmann, PhD • Associate Professor of Physics • University of St. Thomas

visit us at www.abdopublishing.com

Published by Magic Wagon, a division of the ABDO Publishing Group, 8000 West 78th Street, Edina, Minnesota 55439. Copyright © 2009 by Abdo Consulting Group, Inc. International copyrights reserved in all countries. All rights reserved. No part of this book may be reproduced in any form without written permission from the publisher.

Looking Glass Library™ is a trademark and logo of Magic Wagon.

Printed in the United States.

Text by Nadia Higgins
Illustrations by Andrés Martínez Ricci
Edited by Jill Sherman
Interior layout and design by Nicole Brecke
Cover design by Nicole Brecke

Library of Congress Cataloging-in-Publication Data

Higgins, Nadia.
  Electricity is everywhere / by Nadia Higgins ; illustrated by Andrés Martínez Ricci.
     p. cm. — (Science rocks!)
  Includes index.
  ISBN 978-1-60270-276-9
  1. Electricity—Juvenile literature. I. Martínez Ricci, Andrés. II. Title.
  QC527.2.H62 2009
  537—dc22
                    2008001611

Table of Contents

Electricity at Work

Flip! What lights your light? *Pop!* What toasts your toast? *Whizzz. Whirrrrl. Vrooom.* What gets machines moving?

Electricity!

From the Power Plant

Electricity is a form of energy. Where does it come from?

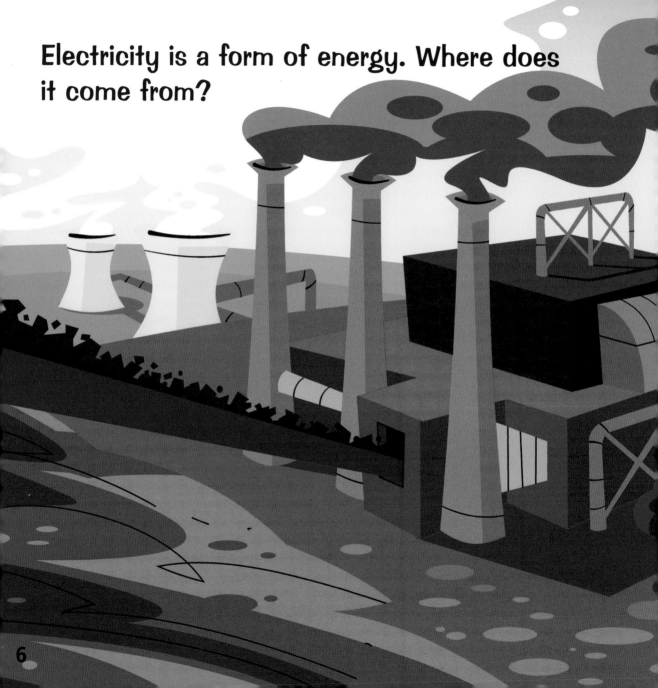

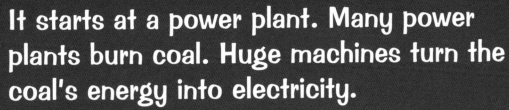

It starts at a power plant. Many power plants burn coal. Huge machines turn the coal's energy into electricity.

Yuck! Burning coal pollutes the air. By saving electricity, you can help keep the air clean. So, remember to turn off lights you are not using!

Electricity flows through wires like water flows through pipes. Thick wires carry electricity from the power plant into town.

Keep away! The wires can be deadly.

Do not climb power poles or trees near them. Don't fly a kite or a remote-controlled airplane near power wires.

Into Your Home

On your street, the wires may be buried underground. Electricity flows up into wires hidden inside your walls. These connect to outlets.

Water is a conductor of electricity. Never use a hair dryer or any other appliance when you are standing in water or have wet hands.

Plug in a radio. Electricity goes up the cord.
It sends out the beat of your favorite song.

Electricity is still not done, though. It travels from the radio back into the outlet. It goes all the way back to the power plant.

Over and over again, electricity moves in a loop called a circuit. Your radio would not play without a circuit.

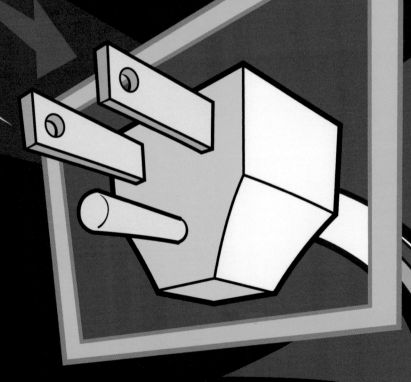

On and Off

Press a button and turn off the TV. What happened?

The button caused a gap in the circuit. Pressing it again turns the TV on. Now the button has closed the gap. Switches and knobs work this way, too.

Inside a Cord

Now look at the TV's cord. It looks like rubber, but rubber only coats the outside. Metal wire runs inside. Why?

The metal is a conductor. Electricity easily flows through it. Electricity can't go through rubber, though. The rubber protects you from a bad electric shock.

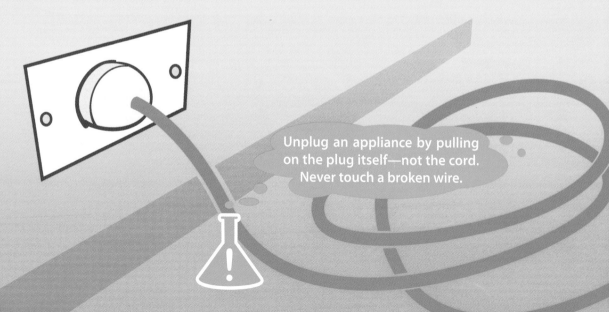

Unplug an appliance by pulling on the plug itself—not the cord. Never touch a broken wire.

Batteries

You don't need a cord to power up, though. You can use batteries instead.

Chemicals inside batteries make electricity that you can carry around.

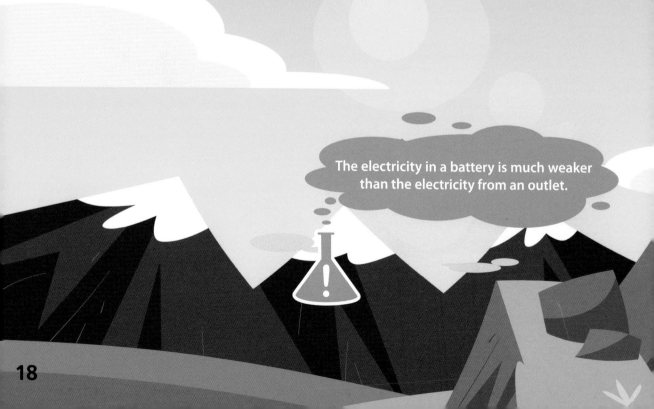

The electricity in a battery is much weaker than the electricity from an outlet.

Static Electricity

Even your body can make electricity. Rub a balloon against your hair. Touch the balloon to the wall. It might just stick!

For a few seconds, static electricity keeps the balloon in place.

If you put the balloon next to a thin stream of running water, the water bends toward it. Try it!

Static electricity happens when certain kinds of materials rub against each other.

Has your hair ever crackled as you combed it? Have you ever touched a friend and felt a shock? That was static electricity!

Lightning

During a thunderstorm, raindrops in a cloud rub together. Static electricity builds up. Flash! Lightning jumps from cloud to cloud or to the ground.

Lightning is a powerful spark of electricity.

The safest place during a thunderstorm is inside a house or a car. Get out of a lake or ocean at the first signs that lightning may be on the way.

25

Power Outage!

Sometimes lightning strikes a power line. It's a power outage! Your whole neighborhood loses electricity.

You have to wait for the electric company to repair the line.

Heavy snow or a fallen tree can snap a power line, too. If you see a fallen power line outside, stay away. Call 9-1-1 to report the fallen line right away.

A power outage gives you a taste of what it was like before people used electricity. Now electricity is everywhere!

Electricity even flows through your body. Electric signals from your brain tell your heart when to beat.

Activity

Climbing Gelatin

What you need:

One tablespoon unflavored gelatin powder

A balloon

A wool hat or sweater

A paper plate

What to do:

1. Sprinkle the gelatin powder on the paper plate.

2. Blow up the balloon and tie the end.

3. Rub the wool on the balloon.

4. Slowly bring the balloon close to the plate, but don't let the two touch.

5. Watch what happens! Static electricity pulls the powder toward the balloon.

Fun Facts

Some power plants use the energy in a waterfall to make electricity. Electricity can also be made from sunlight or spinning windmills. These energy sources don't pollute the air or use up precious fuels such as coal and oil.

Electricity on a spacecraft is made from sunlight. Solar panels on the craft turn the sun's energy into electricity.

Have you ever plugged something in and suddenly lost power? Having too many appliances running at once can overload the wires in your home, making them dangerously hot. A fuse or a circuit breaker is a safety feature that shuts off the power and prevents overheating from happening. You have to change the fuse or flip the circuit breaker to get power back.

In colonial America, lightning caused many fires. Benjamin Franklin invented the lightning rod. It is a metal rod placed on top of a roof that sends lightning safely into the ground. Franklin's invention prevented many fires.

Lightning can heat the air around it to 50,000 degrees Fahrenheit (28,000°C). That's about five times hotter than the surface of the sun!

The first power plants started making electricity in the 1880s. These power plants provided electricity to just a few buildings. During the 1900s, the demand for electricity skyrocketed with the invention of electrical devices such as radios, televisions, telephones, and computers. Today a single power plant can provide electricity for thousands of homes.

Glossary

circuit—a loop that electricity must travel in order to work.

conductor—material that electricity can travel through.

energy—power from electricity that can make light, heat, or motion.

static electricity—electricity that builds up by rubbing certain materials together.

On the Web

To learn more about electricity, visit ABDO Publishing Company on the World Wide Web at **www.abdopublishing.com**. Web sites about electricity are featured on our Book Links page. These links are routinely monitored and updated to provide the most current information available.

Index